The Hagopian Institute, LLC has compiled the _Quote Junkie_ series. The overall series includes over 8,000 quotes, focusing mostly on short quotes that can be used in everyday life as sources of wisdom and inspiration. This particular edition of the series includes quotes about leadership from some of the world's greatest leaders. This edition will prove to be an excellent source of words of wisdom for coaches, teachers, managers, and parents. Please enjoy, and share these quotes with your co-workers, friends and family.

Todd Hagopian

President

The Hagopian Institute, LLC

I0455522

A friend is one who has the same enemies as you have.

Abraham Lincoln

A house divided against itself cannot stand.

Abraham Lincoln

Am I not destroying my enemies when I make friends of them?

Abraham Lincoln

Ballots are the rightful and peaceful successors to bullets.

Abraham Lincoln

Don't worry when you are not recognized, but strive to be worthy of recognition

Abraham Lincoln

Everybody likes a compliment.

Abraham Lincoln

He has a right to criticize, who has a heart to help.

Abraham Lincoln

I do not think much of a man who is not wiser today than he was yesterday

Abraham Lincoln

I never had a policy; I have just tried to do my very best each and every day.

Abraham Lincoln

I walk slowly, but I never walk backward.

Abraham Lincoln

I will prepare and some day my chance will come.

Abraham Lincoln

Let not him who is houseless pull down the house of another, but let him work diligently and build one for himself, thus by example assuring that his own shall be safe from violence when built.

Abraham Lincoln

My great concern is not whether you have failed, but whether you are content with your failure.

Abraham Lincoln

Some single mind must be master, else there will be no agreement in anything.

Abraham Lincoln

Things may come to those who wait, but only the things left by those who hustle.

Abraham Lincoln

Those who deny freedom to others deserve it not for themselves.

Abraham Lincoln

To sin by silence when they should protest makes cowards of men.

Abraham Lincoln

When I do good, I feel good. When I do bad, I feel bad. That's my religion.

Abraham Lincoln

What we have done for ourselves alone dies with us; what we have done for others and the world remains and is immortal.

Albert Pike

A man should live with his superiors as he does with his fire: not too near, lest he burn; nor too far off, lest he freeze.

Albert Pike

Instinct is untaught ability.

Alexander Bain

There is nothing impossible to him who will try.

Alexander The Great

Liberty cannot be preserved, if the manners of the people are corrupted.

Algernon Sydney

It is always the simple that produces the marvelous.

Amelia Barr

It is only in sorrow bad weather masters us; in joy we face the storm and defy it.

Amelia Barr

Surplus wealth is a sacred trust which its possessor is bound to administer in his lifetime for the good of the community.

Andrew Carnegie

No man will make a great leader who wants to do it all himself or get all the credit for doing it.

Andrew Carnegie

The secret of success lies not in doing your own work, but in recognizing the right man to do it.

Andrew Carnegie

If you want to be happy, set a goal that commands your thoughts, liberates your energy, and inspires your hopes.

Andrew Carnegie

You cannot push anyone up the ladder unless he is willing to climb.

Andrew Carnegie

If I am shot at, I want no man to be in the way of the bullet.

Andrew Johnson

Observe your enemies, for they first find out your faults.

Antisthenes

All men by nature desire knowledge.

Aristotle

Change in all things is sweet.

Aristotle

Character may almost be called the most effective means of persuasion.

Aristotle

Dignity consists not in possessing honors, but in the consciousness that we deserve them.

Aristotle

He who is to be a good ruler must have first been ruled.

Aristotle

It is the mark of an educated mind to be able to entertain a thought without accepting it.

Aristotle

No one loves the man whom he fears.

Aristotle

The whole is more than the sum of its parts.

Aristotle

Those that know, do. Those that understand, teach.

Aristotle

We are what we repeatedly do. Excellence, then, is not an act, but a habit.

Aristotle

Well begun is half done.

Aristotle

What it lies in our power to do, it lies in our power not to do.

Aristotle

Man's action is only a picture book of his creed.

Arthur Helps

I found Rome a city of bricks and left it a city of marble.

Augustus

A wise man gets more use from his enemies than a fool from his friends.

Baltasar Gracian

Be content to act, and leave the talking to others.

Baltasar Gracian

Don't take the wrong side of an argument just because your opponent has taken the right side.

Baltasar Gracian

It is better to sleep on things beforehand than lie awake about them afterwards.

Baltasar Gracian

It is good to vary in order that you may frustrate the curious, especially those who envy you.

Baltasar Gracian

Know or listen to those who know.

Baltasar Gracian

Never contend with a man who has nothing to lose.

Baltasar Gracian

Quit while you're ahead. All the best gamblers do.

Baltasar Gracian

The wise does at once what the fool does at last.

Baltasar Gracian

Those who insist on the dignity of their office show they have not deserved it.

Baltasar Gracian

Work is the price which is paid for reputation.

Baltasar Gracian

In most things success depends on knowing how long it takes to succeed.

Baron de Montesquieu

There is no crueler tyranny than that which is perpetuated under the shield of law and in the name of justice.

Baron de Montesquieu

To become truly great, one has to stand with people, not above them.

Baron de Montesquieu

The greatest good you can do for another is not just share your riches, but to reveal to him his own.

Benjamin Disraeli

Taking a new step, uttering a new word, is what people fear most.

Benjamin Disraeli

Either write something worth reading or do something worth writing.

Benjamin Franklin

He that is good for making excuses is seldom good for anything else.

Benjamin Franklin

If you would persuade, you must appeal to interest rather than intellect.

Benjamin Franklin

Never leave that till tomorrow which you can do today.

Benjamin Franklin

Never confuse motion with action.

Benjamin Franklin

Do not fear mistakes. You will know failure. Continue to reach out.

Benjamin Franklin

Energy and persistence conquer all things.

Benjamin Franklin

If passion drives you, let reason hold the reins.

Benjamin Franklin

He that cannot obey, cannot command.

Benjamin Franklin

We must all hang together, or assuredly, we shall all hang separately.

Benjamin Franklin

If there be any truer measure of a man than by what he does, it must be by what he gives.

Bishop Robert Smith

Defeat should never be a source of discouragement, but rather a fresh stimulus.

Bishop Robert Smith

The way to have power is to take it.

Boss Tweed

Never let a day pass that you will have cause to say, I will do better tomorrow.

Brigham Young

All that we are is the result of what we have thought. The mind is everything. What we think we become.

Buddha

An idea that is developed and put into action is more important than an idea that exists only as an idea.

Buddha

He is able who thinks he is able.

Buddha

I do not believe in a fate that falls on men however they act; but I do believe in a fate that falls on them unless they act.

Buddha

I never see what has been done; I only see what remains to be done.

Buddha

It is a man's own mind, not his enemy or foe, that lures him to evil ways.

Buddha

No one saves us but ourselves. No one can and no one may. We ourselves must walk the path.

Buddha

The mind is everything. What you think you become.

Buddha

There are only two mistakes one can make along the road to truth; not going all the way, and not starting.

Buddha

No person was ever honored for what he received. Honor has been the reward for what he gave.

Calvin Coolidge

Heroism is not only in the man, but in the occasion.

Calvin Coolidge

We cannot do everything at once, but we can do something at once.

Calvin Coolidge

Don't expect to build up the weak by pulling down the strong.

Calvin Coolidge

In life, as in chess, forethought wins.

Charles Buxton

Look twice before you leap.

Charlotte Bronte

I am tired of talk that comes to nothing.

Chief Joseph

I believe much trouble would be saved if we opened our hearts more.

Chief Joseph

I will speak with a straight tongue

Chief Joseph

Wherever you go, go with all your heart.

Confucius

A superior man is modest in his speech, but exceeds in his actions.

Confucius

It does not matter how slowly you go so long as you do not stop.

Confucius

Faced with what is right, to leave it undone shows a lack of courage.

Confucius

The superior man acts before he speaks, and afterwards speaks according to his action.

Confucius

To be wronged is nothing unless you continue to remember it.

Confucius

When you are laboring for others let it be with the same zeal as if it were for yourself.

Confucius

You have undertaken to cheat me. I won't sue you, for the law is too slow. I will ruin you.

Cornelius Vanderbilt

And what is the greatest number? Number one.

David Hume

Good means not merely not to do wrong, but rather not to desire to do wrong.

Democritus

It is better to destroy one's own errors than those of others.

Democritus

Our sins are more easily remembered than our good deeds.

Democritus

A good portion of speaking will consist in knowing how to lie.

Desiderius Erasmus

Wise kings generally have wise counselors; and he must be a wise man himself who is capable of distinguishing one.

Diogenes

Do not think you will necessarily be aware of your own enlightenment.

Dogen

I fight fairly, and in good faith.

Edmund About

Where there are many counsellors there is safety.

Edward Coke

A heart to resolve, a head to contrive, and a hand to execute.

Edward Gibbon

Our work is the presentation of our capabilities.

Edward Gibbon

An ounce of loyalty is worth a pound of cleverness.

Elbert Hubbard

The best preparation for good work tomorrow is to do good work today.

Elbert Hubbard

One machine can do the work of fifty ordinary men. No machine can do the work of one extraordinary man.

Elbert Hubbard

The greatest mistake you can make in life is continually fearing that you'll make one.

Elbert Hubbard

The world is moving so fast these days that the man who says it can't be done is generally interrupted by someone doing it.

Elbert Hubbard

A person who has not done one half his day's work by ten o clock, runs a chance of leaving the other half undone.

Emily Bronte

If I could I would always work in silence and obscurity, and let my efforts be known by their results.

Emily Bronte

If evil be spoken of you and it be true, correct yourself, if it be a lie, laugh at it.

Epictetus

If you want to improve, be content to be thought foolish and stupid.

Epictetus

It's not what happens to you, but how you react to it that matters.

Epictetus

Men are disturbed not by things, but by the view which they take of them.

Epictetus

No great thing is created suddenly.

Epictetus

The world turns aside to let any man pass who knows where he is going.

Epictetus

Skillful pilots gain their reputation from storms and tempest.

Epictetus

The greater the difficulty, the more the glory in surmounting it.

Epictetus

How very little can be done under the spirit of fear

Florence Nightingale

I attribute my success to this - I never gave or took any excuse

Florence Nightingale

Affairs that depend on many rarely succeed.

Francesco Guicciardini

A man must make his opportunity, as oft as find it.

Francis Bacon

A prudent question is one-half of wisdom.

Francis Bacon

That action is best which procures the greatest happiness for the greatest numbers.

Francis Hutcheson

That which does not kill us makes us stronger.

Friedrich Nietzsche

Amid the pressure of great events, a general principle gives no help.

Georg Wilhelm Friedrich Hegel

Nothing great in the world has ever been accomplished without passion.

Georg Wilhelm Friedrich Hegel

It is not in the nature of politics that the best men should be elected. The best men do not want to govern their fellowmen.

George Macdonald

It is not the cares of today, but the cares of tomorrow, that weigh a man down.

George Macdonald

To be trusted is a greater complement than to be loved.

George Macdonald

Always imitate the behavior of the winners when you lose.

George Meredith

If we are wise, let us prepare for the worst.

George Washington

Be courteous to all, but intimate with few, and let those few be well tried before you give them your confidence.

George Washington

It is better to offer no excuse than a bad one.

George Washington

Good council has no price.

Giuseppe Mazzini

Slumber not in the tents of your fathers. The world is advancing

Giuseppe Mazzini

Success is a consequence and must not be a goal.

Gustave Flaubert

If at first you do succeed - try to hide your astonishment.

Harry Banks

Clever people will recognize and tolerate nothing but cleverness.

Henri Frederic Amiel

Order is power.

Henri Frederic Amiel

The best path through life is the highway.

Henri Frederic Amiel

To do a common thing uncommonly well brings success.

Henry J Heinz

Heights by great men reached and kept were not obtained by sudden flight but, while their companions slept, they were toiling upward in the night.

Henry Wadsworth Longfellow

Ambition is so powerful a passion in the human breast, that however high we reach we are never satisfied.

Henry Wadsworth Longfellow

He that respects himself is safe from others. He wears a coat of mail that none can pierce.

Henry Wadsworth Longfellow

Look not mournfully into the past, it comes not back again. Wisely improve the present, it is thine. Go forth to meet the shadowy future without fear and with a manly heart.

Henry Wadsworth Longfellow

I never knew an early-rising, hard-working, prudent man, careful of his earnings, and strictly honest who complained of bad luck.

Henry Ward Beecher

He is rich or poor according to what he is, not according to what he has.

Henry Ward Beecher

We should not judge people by their peak of excellence; but by the distance they have traveled from the point where they started.

Henry Ward Beecher

It is not the going out of port, but the coming in, that determines the success of a voyage.

Henry Ward Beecher

It's not the work which kills people, it's the worry. It's not the revolution that destroys machinery it's the friction.

Henry Ward Beecher

Big results require big ambitions.

Heraclitus

No one that encounters prosperity does not also encounter danger.

Heraclitus

He who has never failed somewhere, that man can not be great.

Herman Melville

As the old saw says well: every end does not appear together with its beginning.

Herodotus

Great deeds are usually wrought at great risks.

Herodotus

The most hateful human misfortune is for a wise man to have no influence.

Herodotus

It is easy to sit up and take notice, What is difficult is getting up and taking action.

Honore de Balzac

Power is not revealed by striking hard or often, but by striking true.

Honore de Balzac

Time is everything; five minutes make the difference between victory and defeat.

Horatio Nelson

First gain the victory and then make the best use of it you can.

Horatio Nelson

Desperate affairs require desperate measures.

Horatio Nelson

To be is to do.

Immanuel Kant

I agree with no one's opinion. I have some of my own.

Ivan Turgenev

Go as far as you can see; when you get there, you'll be able to see farther.

J.P. Morgan

No problem can be solved until it is reduced to some simple form. The changing of a vague difficulty into a specific, concrete form is a very essential element in thinking.

J.P. Morgan

Affluence means influence.

Jack London

Superior strength is found in the long run to lie with those who had right on their side.

James Anthony Froude

The practical effect of a belief is the real test of its soundness.

James Anthony Froude

The test of leadership is not to put greatness into humanity, but to elicit it, for the greatness is already there.

James Buchanan

A brave man is a man who dares to look the Devil in the face and tell him he is a Devil.

James Garfield

I mean to make myself a man, and if I succeed in that, I shall succeed in everything else.

James Garfield

All men having power ought to be distrusted to a certain degree.

James Madison

A little flattery will support a man through great fatigue.

James Monroe

I do not say that, when brought to the test, I shall be invincible.

James Otis

The giving is the hardest part; what does it cost to add a smile?

Jean de la Bruyere

A position of eminence makes a great person greater and a small person less.

Jean de la Bruyere

A vain man finds it wise to speak good or ill of himself; a modest man does not talk of himself.

Jean de la Bruyere

It is a sad thing when men have neither the wit to speak well nor the judgment to hold their tongues.

Jean de la Bruyere

Courage consists not in blindly overlooking danger, but in seeing it, and conquering it.

Jean Paul

Be great in act, as you have been in thought.

Jean Paul

You prove your worth with your actions, not with your mouth.

Jean Paul

When something an affliction happens to you, you either let it defeat you, or you defeat it.

Jean-Jacques Rousseau

He who seldom speaks, and with one calm well-timed word can strike dumb the loquacious, is a genius or a hero.

Johann Kaspar Lavater

A good idea plus capable men cannot fail; it is better than money in the bank.

John Berry

And, if there was any responsibility in refusing to obey, he was willing to accept it.

John Bigelow

An executive is a person who always decides sometimes he decides correctly, but he always decides.

John Henry Patterson

Before you try to convince anyone else, be sure you are convinced, and if you cannot convince yourself, drop the subject.

John Henry Patterson

To listen well is as powerful a means of communication and influence as to talk well.

John Marshall

If your actions inspire others to dream more, learn more, do more and become more, you are a leader.

John Quincy Adams

I am not aware that any community has a right to force another to be civilized.

John Stuart Mill

One person with a belief is equal to a force of ninety-nine who have only interest.

John Stuart Mill

What distinguishes the majority of men from the few is their inability to act according to their beliefs.

John Stuart Mill

To be able to bear provocation is an argument of great reason, and to forgive it of a great mind.

John Tillotson

It's easy to work for somebody else; all you have to do is show up.

John Wanamaker

Keep up the old standards, and day by day raise them higher.

John Wanamaker

Vision is the art of seeing what is invisible to others.

Jonathan Swift

Discovery consists of seeing what everybody has seen and thinking what nobody else has thought.

Jonathan Swift

Blessed is he who expects nothing, for he shall never be disappointed.

Jonathan Swift

It is a sin not to do what one is capable of doing.

Jose Marti

An insatiable appetite for glory leads to sacrifice and death, but innate instinct leads to self-preservation and life.

Jose Marti

One just principle from the depths of a cave is more powerful than an army

Jose Marti

A feeble executive implies a feeble execution of the government.

Joseph Story

One of rarest things that a man ever does is to do the best he can.

Josh Billings

You are one of the forces of nature.

Jules Michelet

I came, I saw, I conquered.

Julius Caesar

I have lived long enough both in years and in accomplishments.

Julius Caesar

I love the name of honor, more than I fear death.

Julius Caesar

No one is so brave that he is not disturbed by something unexpected.

Julius Caesar

Which death is preferably to every other? "The unexpected".

Julius Caesar

For the bureaucrat, the world is a mere object to be manipulated by him.

Karl Marx

It is even better to act quickly and err than to hesitate until the time of action is past.

Karl Von Clausewitz

Now that I am a deputy, I will cease to be an agitator.

Lajos Kossuth

When the best leader's work is done the people say, "We did it ourselves."

Lao Tzu

When I let go of what I am, I become what I might be.

Lao Tzu

To see things in the seed, that is genius.

Lao Tzu

One who is too insistent on his own views, finds few to agree with him.

Lao Tzu

Nature does not hurry, yet everything is accomplished.

Lao Tzu

Govern a great nation as you would cook a small fish. Do not overdo it.

Lao Tzu

Give a man a fish and you feed him for a day. Teach him how to fish and you feed him for a lifetime.

Lao Tzu

Anticipate the difficult by managing the easy.

Lao Tzu

An ant on the move does more than a dozing ox.

Lao Tzu

Nothing is so perfectly amusing as a total change of ideas.

Laurence Sterne

The desire of knowledge, like the thirst of riches, increases ever with the acquisition of it.

Laurence Sterne

Titles of honor are like the impressions on coins, which add no value to gold or silver, but only render brass current.

Laurence Sterne

The great recipe for success is to work, and always work.

Leon Gambetta

People may doubt what you say, but they will believe what you do.

Lewis Cass

Compromise: An agreement between two men to do what both agree is wrong.

Lord Edward Gascoyne-Cecil

Do the things you know, and you shall learn the truth you need to know.

Louisa May Alcott

He who believes is strong; he who doubts is weak. Strong convictions precede great actions.

Louisa May Alcott

The wicked are always surprised to find ability in the good.

Luc de Clapiers

To execute great things, one should live as though one would never die.

Luc de Clapiers

Belief in oneself is one of the most important bricks in building any successful venture.

Lydia Child

It is right noble to fight with wickedness and wrong; the mistake is in supposing that spiritual evil can be overcome by physical means.

Lydia Child

If coming events are said to cast their shadows before, past events cannot fail to leave their impress behind them.

Madame Blavatsky

Your life is what your thoughts make it.

Marcus Aurelius

You have power over your mind - not outside events. Realize this, and you will find strength.

Marcus Aurelius

Waste no more time arguing about what a good man should be. Be one.

Marcus Aurelius

The secret of all victory lies in the organization of the non-obvious.

Marcus Aurelius

That which is not good for the bee-hive cannot be good for the bees.

Marcus Aurelius

Confine yourself to the present.

Marcus Aurelius

Those who understand only what can be explained understand very little.

Marie von Ebner-Eschenbach

Keep away from people who try to belittle your ambitions. Small people always do that, but the really great make you feel that you, too, can become great.

Mark Twain

The right word may be effective, but no word was ever as effective as a rightly timed pause.

Mark Twain

If you tell the truth, you don't have to remember anything.

Mark Twain

It is always by way of pain one arrives at pleasure.

Marquis de Sade

First I shake the whole Apple tree, that the ripest might fall. Then I climb the tree and shake each limb, and then each branch and then each twig, and then I look under each leaf

Martin Luther

Any institution which does not suppose the people good, and the magistrate corruptible, is evil.

Maximilien Robespierre

Do exactly what you would do if you felt most secure.

Meister Eckhart

The price of inaction is far greater than the cost of making a mistake.

Meister Eckhart

Not being able to govern events, I govern myself.

Michel de Montaigne

To be prepared is half the victory.

Miguel de Cervantes

You win battles by knowing the enemy's timing, and using a timing which the enemy does not expect.

Miyamoto Musashi

Perceive that which cannot be seen with the eye.

Miyamoto Musashi

Do nothing which is of no use.

Miyamoto Musashi

A celebrated people lose dignity upon a closer view.

Napolean Bonaparte

A leader is a dealer in hope.

Napolean Bonaparte

A picture is worth a thousand words.

Napolean Bonaparte

Among those who dislike oppression are many who like to oppress.

Napolean Bonaparte

An army marches on its stomach.

Napolean Bonaparte

Courage is like love; it must have hope for nourishment

Napolean Bonaparte

Forethought we may have, undoubtedly, but not foresight.

Napolean Bonaparte

He who fears being conquered is sure of defeat.

Napolean Bonaparte

I am sometimes a fox and sometimes a lion. The whole secret of government lies in knowing when to be the one or the other.

Napolean Bonaparte

I can no longer obey; I have tasted command, and I cannot give it up.

Napolean Bonaparte

I have only one counsel for you - be master.

Napolean Bonaparte

I made all my generals out of mud.

Napolean Bonaparte

If you want a thing done well, do it yourself.

Napolean Bonaparte

Imagination rules the world.

Napolean Bonaparte

Nothing is more difficult, and therefore more precious, than to be able to decide.

Napolean Bonaparte

One should never forbid what one lacks the power to prevent.

Napolean Bonaparte

Power is my mistress. I have worked too hard at her conquest to allow anyone to take her away from me.

Napolean Bonaparte

Public opinion is the thermometer a monarch should constantly consult.

Napolean Bonaparte

Respect the burden.

Napolean Bonaparte

Ten people who speak make more noise than ten thousand who are silent.

Napolean Bonaparte

The act of policing is, in order to punish less often, to punish more severely.

Napolean Bonaparte

The truest wisdom is a resolute determination.

Napolean Bonaparte

To do all that one is able to do, is to be a man; to do all that one would like to do, is to be a god.

Napolean Bonaparte

Victory belongs to the most persevering.

Napolean Bonaparte

When small men attempt great enterprises, they always end by reducing them to the level of their mediocrity.

Napolean Bonaparte

When soldiers have been baptized in the fire of a battle-field, they have all one rank in my eyes.

Napolean Bonaparte

You must not fear death, my lads; defy him, and you drive him into the enemy's ranks.

Napolean Bonaparte

You must not fight too often with one enemy, or you will teach him all your art of war.

Napolean Bonaparte

Not only strike while the iron is hot, but make it hot by striking.

Oliver Cromwell

Necessity has no law.

Oliver Cromwell

We have met the enemy, and they are ours.

Oliver Perry

A government must not waiver once it has chosen it's course. It must not look to the left or right but go forward.

Otto von Bismarck

Either I will find a way, or I will make one.

Philip Sidney

Wise men talk because they have something to say; fools, because they have to say something.

Plato

Never discourage anyone.....who continually makes progress, no matter how slow.

Plato

The measure of a man is what he does with power.

Plato

Those who know how to win are much more numerous than those who know how to make proper use of their victories.

Polybius

He is not wise to me who is wise in words only, but he who is wise in deeds.

Pope Gregory I

We are not interested in the possibilities of defeat. They do not exist.

Queen Victoria

To know even one life has breathed easier because you have lived. This is to have succeeded.

Ralph Waldo Emerson

Do not follow where the path may lead. Go, instead, where there is no path and leave a trail.

Ralph Waldo Emerson

Everybody keeps telling me how surprised they are with what I've done. But I'm telling you honestly that it doesn't surprise me. I knew I could do it.

Ralph Waldo Emerson

The invariable mark of wisdom is to see the miraculous in the common.

Ralph Waldo Emerson

An ounce of action is worth a ton of theory

Ralph Waldo Emerson

A great man is always willing to be little.

Ralph Waldo Emerson

If you want to go east, don't go west.

Ramakrishna

Change is not made without inconvenience, even from worse to better.

Richard Hooker

I cannot trust a man to control others who cannot control himself.

Robert E. Lee

Never ignore a gut feeling, but never believe that it's enough.

Robert Heller

Courage without conscience is a wild beast.

Robert Ingersoll

Few rich men own their own property. The property owns them.

Robert Ingersoll

The greatest test of courage on earth is to bear defeat without losing heart.

Robert Ingersoll

It is the safeguard of the strongest that he lives under a government which is obliged to respect the voice of the weakest.

Robert Purvis

The leadership has failed. Even so, the leadership can and must be recreated from the masses and out of the masses.

Rosa Luxemburg

In some causes silence is dangerous.

Saint Ambrose

The scars of others should teach us caution.

Saint Jerome

To reach something good it is very useful to have gone astray, and thus acquire experience.

Saint Teresa of Avila

A good man would prefer to be defeated than to defeat injustice by evil means.

Sallust

Ambition breaks the ties of blood, and forgets the obligations of gratitude.

Sallust

Every man is the architect of his own fortune.

Sallust

It is better to use fair means and fail, than foul and conquer.

Sallust

Necessity makes even the timid brave.

Sallust

We employ the mind to rule, the body to serve.

Sallust

Every one, more or less, loves Power, yet those who most wish for it are seldom the fittest to be trusted with it.

Samuel Richardson

Though bitter, good medicine cures illness. Though it may hurt, loyal criticism will have beneficial effects.

Sima Qian

The tyrant dies and his rule is over, the martyr dies and his rule begins.

Soren Kierkegaard

To dare is to lose one's footing momentarily. Not to dare is to lose oneself.

Soren Kierkegaard

Always mystify, mislead and surprise the enemy if possible.

Stonewall Jackson

You have to believe in yourself.

Sun Tzu

Opportunities multiply as they are seized.

Sun Tzu

Invincibility lies in the defense; the possibility of victory in the attack.

Sun Tzu

He that fights and runs away, May turn and fight another day; But he that is in battle slain, Will never rise to fight again.

Tacitus

No one would have doubted his ability to reign had he never been emperor.

Tacitus

Reason and judgment are the qualities of a leader

Tacitus

From my tribe I take nothing, I am the maker of my own fortune.

Tecumseh

The future condition of the conquered power depends on the will of the conquerer.

Thaddeus Stevens

Do what you can, with what you have, where you are.

Theodore Roosevelt

In a moment of decision the best thing you can do is the right thing. The worst thing you can do is nothing.

Theodore Roosevelt

The best executive is the one who has sense enough to pick good men to do what he wants done, and self-restraint to keep from meddling with them while they do it.

Theodore Roosevelt

The most important single ingredient in the formula of success is knowing how to get along with people.

Theodore Roosevelt

Far and away the best prize that life has to offer is the chance to work hard at work worth doing.

Theodore Roosevelt

People ask the difference between a leader and a boss. The leader works in the open, and the boss in covert. The leader leads, and the boss drives.

Theodore Roosevelt

When you are asked if you can do a job, tell 'em, "Certainly I can!" Then get busy and find out how to do it.

Theodore Roosevelt

Great thoughts speak only to the thoughtful mind, but great actions speak to all mankind.

Theodore Roosevelt

A good leader can't get too far ahead of his followers.

Theodore Roosevelt

Courtesy is as much a mark of a gentleman as courage.

Theodore Roosevelt

Nobody cares how much you know, until they know how much you care.

Theodore Roosevelt

To convert somebody go and take them by the hand and guide them.

Thomas Aquinas

A single breaker may recede; but the tide is evidently coming in.

Thomas B. Macaulay

A man lives by believing something: not by debating and arguing about many things.

Thomas Carlyle

A man without a goal is like a ship without a rudder.

Thomas Carlyle

A person who is gifted sees the essential point and leaves the rest as surplus.

Thomas Carlyle

A strong mind always hopes, and has always cause to hope.

Thomas Carlyle

Conviction is worthless unless it is converted into conduct.

Thomas Carlyle

Do the duty which lies nearest to you, the second duty will then become clearer.

Thomas Carlyle

Doubt, of whatever kind, can be ended by action alone.

Thomas Carlyle

Everywhere in life, the true question is not what we gain, but what we do.

Thomas Carlyle

He who could foresee affairs three days in advance would be rich for thousands of years.

Thomas Carlyle

I've got a great ambition to die of exhaustion rather than boredom.

Thomas Carlyle

Men do less than they ought, unless they do all that they can.

Thomas Carlyle

No amount of ability is of the slightest avail without honor.

Thomas Carlyle

Our main business is not to see what lies dimly at a distance,but to do what lies clearly at hand.

Thomas Carlyle

Talk that does not end in any kind of action is better suppressed altogether.

Thomas Carlyle

The first duty of man is to conquer fear; he must get rid of it, he cannot act till then.

Thomas Carlyle

The greatest of all faults, I should say, is to be conscious of none.

Thomas Carlyle

The fool wanders, a wise man travels.

Thomas Fuller

Nothing is easy to the unwilling.

Thomas Fuller

Always mystify, mislead and surprise the enemy if possible.

Thomas J. Jackson

It takes time to persuade men to do even what is for their own good.

Thomas Jefferson

The moment a person forms a theory, his imagination sees in every object only the tracts which favor that theory.

Thomas Jefferson

It is frequently a misfortune to have very brilliant men in charge of affairs. They expect too much of ordinary men.

Thucydides

It becomes an emperor to die standing.

Titus

All our dreams can come true, if we have the courage to pursue them.

Walt Disney

You may not realize it when it happens, but a kick in the teeth may be the best thing in the world for you.

Walt Disney

The way to get started is to quit talking and begin doing.

Walt Disney

If you can dream it, you can do it.

Walt Disney

It's kind of fun to do the impossible.

Walt Disney

Get a good idea and stay with it. Do it, and work at it until it's done right.

Walt Disney

A person should set his goals as early as he can and devote all his energy and talent to getting there. With enough effort, he may achieve it. Or he may find something that is even more rewarding.

Walt Disney

Do what you do so well that they will want to see it again and bring their friends

Walt Disney

For success, attitude is equally as important as ability.

Walter Scott

Success - keeping your mind awake and your desire asleep.

Walter Scott

Great minds have purposes; others have wishes.

Washington Irving

The easiest thing to do, whenever you fail, is to put yourself down by blaming your lack of ability for your misfortunes.

Washington Irving

Little minds are tamed and subdued by misfortune; but great minds rise above them.

Washington Irving

Many know how to flatter, few know how to praise.

Wendell Phillips

The keener the want the lustier the growth.

Wendell Phillips

The greatness of a man's power is the measure of his surrender.

William Booth

We must wake ourselves up! Or somebody else will take our place, and bear our cross, and thereby rob us of our crown.

William Booth

The one thing you can't do when you're highly ranked is relax.

William Floyd

Tact is one of the first mental virtues, the absence of it is fatal to the best talent.

William Gilmore Simms

You cannot fight against the future. Time is on our side.

William Gladstone

It is always well to get near to men of genius.

William Henry Moody

Begin to be now what you will be hereafter.

William James

Nothing is so fatiguing as the eternal hanging on of an uncompleted task.

William James

Pessimism leads to weakness, optimism to power.

William James

In the time of darkest defeat, victory may be nearest.

William McKinley

That's all a man can hope for during his lifetime - to set an example - and when he is dead, to be an inspiration for history.

William McKinley

Knowledge is the treasure of a wise man.

William Penn

O Lord, help me not to despise or oppose what I do not understand.

William Penn

Rarely promise, but, if lawful, constantly perform.

William Penn

Time is what we want most, but what we use worst.

William Penn

Unlimited power corrupts the possessor.

William Pitt

Strong reasons make strong actions.

William Shakespeare

If nominated, I will not run; if elected, I will not serve.

William Tecumseh Sherman

We come to beginnings only at the end.

William Throsby Bridges

People don't follow titles, they follow courage.

William Wells Brown

The sweetest of all sounds is praise.

Xenophon

I have always done my duty. I am ready to die. My only regret is for the friends I leave behind me.

Zachary Taylor

www.ingramcontent.com/pod-product-compliance
Lightning Source LLC
Chambersburg PA
CBHW052011280526

45793CB00005B/928